# Table of Contents

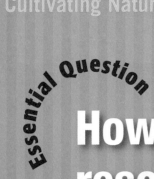

Essential Question

# How do we decide which resources we should develop?

# The Structure of a Corn Plant

by Mark Felkonian

Notes

1    Maize, often called corn, is a plant species that is native to North America. First cultivated thousands of years ago by the early inhabitants of what is now Mexico, corn is an adaptable plant that can grow in different types of climates. As people migrated, they grew corn in other regions. As a result, the crop soon spread across the continent.

2    Over time, humans developed varieties of corn plants for different uses. Today, corn is a major food source for humans and livestock (the animals humans raise in order to eat). It is also used to make medicine, to preserve food, and to fuel engines.

3    Corn is a tall, green, leafy plant most often supported by a single stem, or stalk, that grows straight upward from a shallow root system in the ground. A typical corn plant will grow as tall as ten feet and have as many as twenty leaves. The leaves grow from nodes that encircle the stalk. Each corn plant has female and male organs, or parts. The female organ is called an ear. The male organ is called the tassel.

4    The ear usually grows out from a leaf node in the middle of the stalk. The ear contains a cylinder, called a cob. The cob has rows of ovules, or eggs. The cob is enclosed in a leafy wrapping called a husk. A soft, thin, hairlike structure called a corn silk will grow from each egg. While the ear is forming, the silks will grow about an inch a day and emerge from the top of the husk.

5    The tassel grows from the top of the plant after all the leaves have sprouted. The tassel is a group of thin branches with many small male flowers that release pollen.

6    When pollen grains from the tassel fall on the exposed silks of the corn ear, pollination occurs. The male cells in the pollen grow along each silk to fertilize the female cells, or eggs. After fertilization, the rows of eggs grow into kernels. A single ear can grow up to three inches in diameter and eight inches in length, and yield anywhere from 500 to 1,000 kernels. Each kernel is a single embryo that contains a new plant.

## The Corn Plant

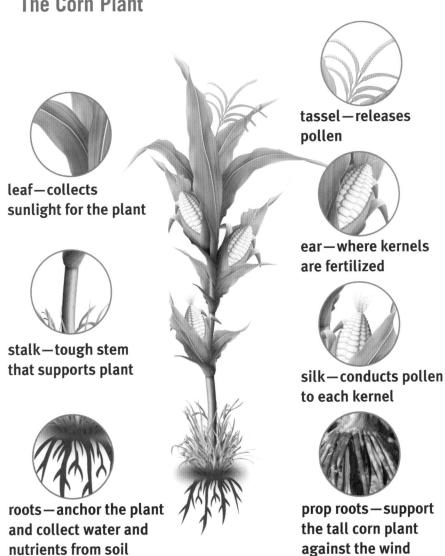

leaf—collects
sunlight for the plant

stalk—tough stem
that supports plant

roots—anchor the plant
and collect water and
nutrients from soil

tassel—releases
pollen

ear—where kernels
are fertilized

silk—conducts pollen
to each kernel

prop roots—support
the tall corn plant
against the wind

Notes

# The Past and Future of a Crop

by Amelia Millilo, Kelly Gold, and Brett Berger

1     Earth is a system in which energy from the sun constantly cycles living and nonliving matter. This happens through various processes. For example, plants, such as corn, are called producers. They use the sun's energy to make food through a chemical process known as photosynthesis. Animals, such as humans, are called consumers. They eat plants (and other animals that have consumed plants) in order to obtain the energy they need to function.

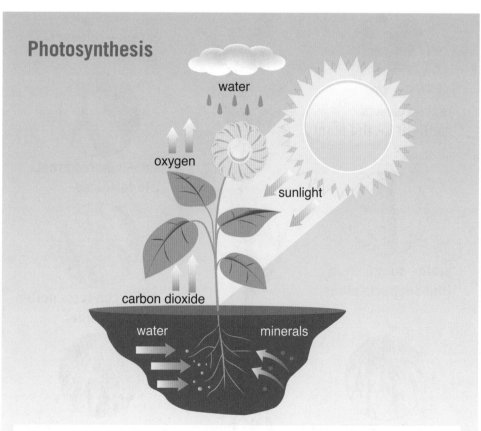

**Photosynthesis**

water

oxygen

sunlight

carbon dioxide

water

minerals

Through photosynthesis, plants combine carbon dioxide and water in the presence of sunlight. This makes glucose, a type of sugar the plant can store and use as food.

Notes

2     Before the emergence of civilizations, early humans hunted and gathered food. As people learned to grow crops for consumption, their relationship to these organisms changed. In the past they simply gathered whatever was growing and ate it. Through cultivation, humans learned to grow certain plants. They slowly developed an understanding of how to breed certain seeds to yield more productive and desirable crops for consumption.

## Plant Energy

3     Corn is one such crop that has been cultivated over time to produce optimum traits for survival and use. Today, corn is a major crop. It is used to feed humans and livestock. Therefore, corn is grown directly to provide humans with food energy—and has been for thousands of years.

4     However, that is not the only kind of energy that corn provides. Over the past century, corn has also been processed into ethanol, a biofuel. It is burned to generate heat energy. This heat energy is in turn converted into a way to power car engines. The United States is the leading nation in corn production. There, more corn is used for ethanol than for food products.

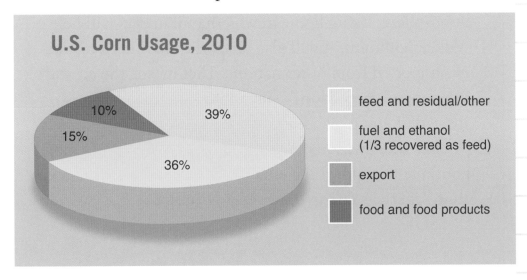

U.S. Corn Usage, 2010

10%    39%    15%    36%

- feed and residual/other
- fuel and ethanol (1/3 recovered as feed)
- export
- food and food products

# The Ethanol Debate

5    In the United States, the issue of how corn crops are used has become a public debate. Should corn be grown as a food? Or as an alternative fuel source? Both sides give an earful in the following two opinion pieces.

## Clean-Burning Corn Is America's Future
by Kelly Gold

6    America's energy consumption is at a record high. As the nation's dependency on fossil fuels increases, Americans have to make a bigger investment in alternative fuel technology and resources. One fuel source that stands out as a solution is ethanol, the corn-based biofuel. But only if American growers continue to support this new industry.

7    There are a few good reasons why America should continue to devote its corn crops to ethanol production. The first is the sheer abundance of corn. In the United States, the world's leading producer of corn, ethanol is a sustainable resource that could continue to meet the country's energy needs well into the future.

8    Another reason is the environment. Ethanol makes a cleaner-burning fuel. This reduces carbon emissions in the atmosphere. Using homegrown ethanol in cars will help reduce pollution. It will also offset the amount of oil and gas imported from other nations. That means the air stays cleaner and more money stays with American farmers instead of going overseas.

9    For these reasons, America and its corn farmers must continue to support the ethanol industry, and at the same time America's energy-independent future.

# Keep Corn on the Cob—Not in My Car!
by Brett Berger

10    Ethanol is not the perfect energy source some would have us believe. Ethanol is not the solution. It is part of the problem. America's corn farmers must get back to putting food on the table while scientists focus on finding a better solution to America's energy needs.

11    The fact is that every bushel of corn made into ethanol is a bushel of corn that can't be eaten by people. Increasing the amount of corn devoted to ethanol will result in increasing food costs. That can endanger the nation's food supply. Currently, only about 10 percent of U.S.-grown corn is sold for human consumption (and much of that is in the form of the sweetener high-fructose corn syrup).

12    Ethanol is also far less friendly to the environment than it is portrayed. True, burning ethanol may cause less harmful emissions than burning gasoline. However, the large-scale farming and manufacturing practices of ethanol production are depleting freshwater resources in the Midwest and severely polluting the soil, water, and air. The use of high-nitrogen fertilizers strips the soil of key nutrients. That upsets the ecosystem and destroys the soil. That could lead to food shortages in the future.

13    America's corn crop is the most productive in the world, yet it's being used to feed cars instead of people. Scientists are trying to figure out how to use the cornstalks and clippings for ethanol, leaving the kernels for food. Until we find a way to make ethanol production green, let's shift corn crops away from biofuel. Let's generate more food for the world. This would keep the corn on the cob, where it belongs, and out of car engines.

Remember to annotate as you read.

Notes

# Paul Bunyan and the Great Popcorn Blizzard

1    Way back in the olden days, Paul Bunyan traveled through the great Midwest with his sidekick, Babe the Blue Ox. At that time, the land was covered with forests as far as the eye could see. Pioneers wanted to settle and farm the land, so Paul and Babe helped them out. The two began to clear the woods.

2    With one swing of Paul's mighty ax, more than a dozen trees would fall like dominoes. Then Babe would haul away the logs that would later be used to build homes. Soon Paul was hiring hundreds of men to help him clear the Midwestern forests. He and his men called themselves lumberjacks.

3    One spring, Paul and his team cleared giant oak trees from the forests of Iowa so that farmers could plant corn. When summer came, the weather was so hot you could fry eggs on a rock. The cornstalks grew as tall as trees. The corn kernels grew so large they looked like balloons about to burst. Paul's lumberjacks complained that it was much too hot to work.

4    On a scorching day, when the temperature was above 110 degrees, the corn started popping! All across Iowa, corn kernels popped out of their ears. Soon the entire state was covered with popcorn thirteen feet deep!

5    The lumberjacks thought it was a snowstorm. They ran inside, put on their jackets and gloves, and came back out to play in the snow! They made snowmen out of popcorn and had popcorn fights. Later on, the men had a good laugh when they realized that during the Great Popcorn Blizzard, everyone forgot how hot it really was!

# BuildReflectWrite

## Build Knowledge

Use the illustration on page 6 to explain photosynthesis. Then, answer the following questions: Which statistic from the pie chart on page 7 would you select to support Kelly Gold's opinion? Why? Brett Berger's? Why?

| Photosynthesis | U.S. Corn Usage, 2010 |
|---|---|
| | **Kelly Gold** |
| | **Brett Berger** |

## Reflect

**How do we decide which resources we should develop?**

Based on this week's texts, write down new ideas and questions you have about the essential question.

_____

_____

_____

_____

_____

_____

## Building Research Skills

**Narrative**

Imagine that you want to write a historical fiction story about how Native Americans taught the first European settlers to grow corn. To develop background knowledge, you must answer this guiding research question: When and where did Native Americans first teach European settlers to grow corn? Read and take notes from two or more sources to find facts and details to answer this question. List your sources.

Remember to annotate as you read.

# A Short History of a Special Plant

by Laura McDonald

1    Today, corn is the largest crop grown in the United States. Most years, American farmers produce more than 60 billion dollars worth of corn. The story of how the United States became the biggest corn producer in the world begins thousands of years ago . . . in what is now Mexico.

2    Corn as we know it today started out as a wild grass plant called teosinte (tay-oh-SIN-tee). More than five thousand years ago, Native Americans in Mexico developed teosinte into maize, or corn. Teosinte has only five to twelve kernels on each ear, while modern corn has hundreds of kernels. Maize spread through North, Central, and South America and became a major part of the Native American diet.

Native Americans began cultivating corn more than five thousand years ago.

3    Maize was an important crop to the first peoples of Central and North America. Most people used every part of the corn. They used the stalks for roofs. The cobs were used for fuel. They used the silk to fill beds. They braided the husks to make mats, beds, baskets, and dolls. The kernels were ground into cornmeal for cooking and baking.

# Early Cultivation

4    The first Native American corn farmers used the seeds from the healthiest corn plants to grow their crops. This selective breeding improved their crop yield. When farmers realized that they could plant a surplus of corn and not hurt their fields, they grew larger crops and stored the leftover corn as a food supply that could last during the winter months. The Native American planting system was called the "Three Sisters" method. For centuries, early farmers planted their fields with three plants—corn, squash, and beans—together. Each plant helped the other grow, and the mixture of plants helped preserve nutrients in the soil.

5    The advantage of planting the three crops together was tenfold. Corn was a strong and vertical plant that stood straight, so the beans could curl up around its stalk. In turn, the beans fixed nitrogen in their roots, helping restore the soil. Meanwhile, the squash leaves spread out on the ground and retained moisture in the soil for the other plants. They also helped keep away pests. This mutually beneficial arrangement among the plants mimics the type of symbiosis found in nature. The end result was a healthy crop that yielded a variety of nutritious plants and also maintained the integrity of the soil.

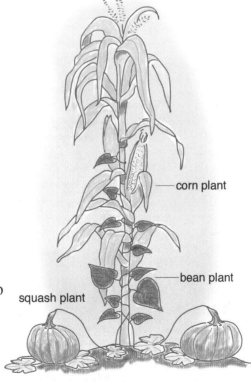

corn plant

bean plant

squash plant

**"Three Sisters" planting mound**

13

6   When European settlers arrived in North America in the 1600s, maize was entirely foreign to them. The English called it "corn" because that is what they called all wheat and barley crops in England. Native Americans taught the settlers how to grow and care for the three sisters crops.

7   Settlers quickly recognized that the corn crop was key to their survival. Using the varieties that had been developed by Native Americans, they began to further breed and cultivate corn types that matured faster and produced even greater yields. Soon, people around the world began to grow and eat maize.

Modern corn is harvested with a combine.

For many centuries, Navaho women harvested corn by hand.

# The Corn Belt

8    In the United States, most of the corn was, and still is, grown in the Midwest, or Corn Belt. This region's climate has the hot summers and regular rainfall that corn needs to grow 3 meters (10 feet) tall.

9    In the past, if a farmer grew corn year after year in the same field, the soil would get worn out and the corn harvest would get smaller and smaller. To combat this problem, farmers rotated crops, planting different crops each year. One common pattern, or rotation, of crops is to plant soybeans one year and corn the next. Soybean plants add nutrients back into the soil.

10    Many farms in the Corn Belt also raised cattle or hogs. These animals eat both corn and cornstalks. In the fall, farmers put animals out in the fields to eat any leftover corn. The animals' wastes help fertilize the ground for the next season.

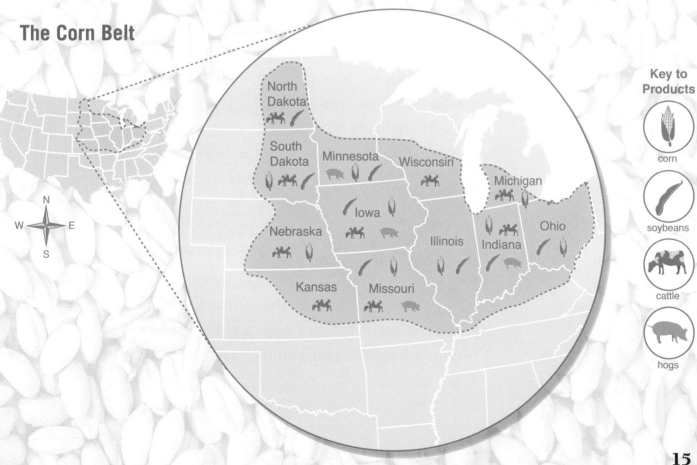

**The Corn Belt**

**Key to Products**

corn

soybeans

cattle

hogs

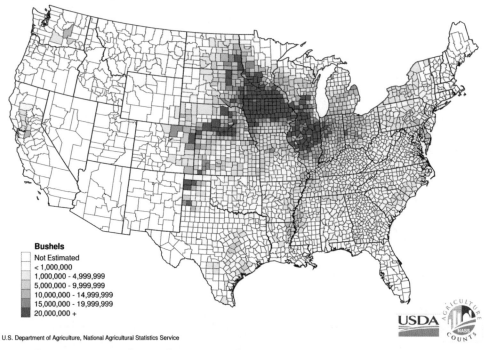

## Corn for Grain 2010 Production by County for Selected States

**Bushels**

- Not Estimated
- < 1,000,000
- 1,000,000 - 4,999,999
- 5,000,000 - 9,999,999
- 10,000,000 - 14,999,999
- 15,000,000 - 19,999,999
- 20,000,000 +

USDA

U.S. Department of Agriculture, National Agricultural Statistics Service

## The Rise of Industrial Farming

11    With industrialization in the 1800s, new farming methods and technology began to change agriculture. American farmers continued to strive to grow strong, healthy corn plants that yield as much as possible. In the late 1800s scientists developed hybrid corn. Fertilizing one variety of corn with pollen from another variety makes hybrids. The result is a new type of corn plant that is stronger and able to produce more seeds than either parent plant. This corn mixed favorable genetic traits and led to healthier varieties of corn and higher, faster yields.

12    As more farmers used hybrid corn, production rose. In 1933 the average yield was 33 bushels per acre. In 1997 the yield had increased to 127 bushels per acre. Today, corn is a staple crop of the Midwestern United States. Ninety-five percent of corn acreage is planted with hybrid corn, and the average annual yield is nearly 159 bushels per acre.

13    Almost all corn in the United States grows from hybrid seeds. Hybrid corn may even contain genetic material, or DNA, from other species altogether. Scientists have added DNA that makes GMO[1] corn more resistant to insects and drought.

14    According to the National Corn Growers of America (NCGA), more than 300 million metric tons of corn are harvested each year in the United States. However, today's industrial farming practices have led to a monoculture where growers raise one type of crop year after year. The success of hybrid corn and soybeans has led many growers to solely raise one cash crop instead of a variety.

15    This is good practice for earning money now. However, it could hurt profits and productivity in the future. The concentration on a single crop depletes the soil. The lack of variety is at odds with how soil functions and maintains balance. The invasion of one disease or pest could wipe out all of the corn crops.

1 GMO—genetically modified organism

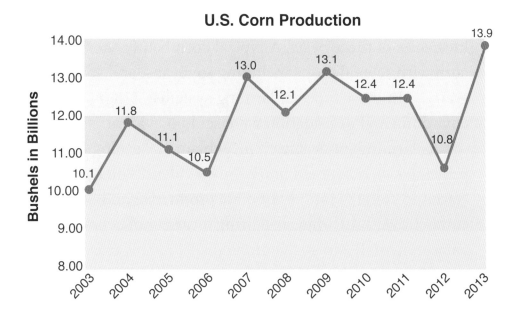

**U.S. Corn Production**

The United States is the largest corn producer in the world.

## Monoculture Pros and Cons

| Advantages | Disadvantages |
| --- | --- |
| • Reduced plant competition | • Increased vulnerability to pests (increased need for insecticide) |
| • Control of unprofitable organisms | • Increased vulnerability to disease outbreaks |
| • Reduction of costs by limitation of specialized machinery | • Erosion and fertility affected by nutrient depletion of soil |
| • Maximization of profit from the growing of high gross margin crops | • Lack of biodiversity at odds with system balance<br>• Nutrient runoff more likely to pollute groundwater supplies |

16    As Miguel A. Altieri, an insect biologist at UC Berkeley, explains: "Until about four decades ago … yields were modest, but stable. Production was safeguarded by growing more than one crop or variety in space and time in a field as insurance against pest outbreaks or severe weather. Inputs of nitrogen were gained by rotating major field crops with legumes. In turn, rotations suppressed insects, weeds, and diseases by effectively breaking the life cycles of these pests. A typical corn belt farmer rotated corn with several crops including soybeans, and small grain … In these types of farming systems … signs of environmental degradation were seldom evident."

17    As farming modernized, he explained, "ecological principles were ignored and/or overridden." Today, "farming systems [are] extremely productive and competitive, [but] they also bring a variety of economic, environmental, and social problems." For this reason, many biologists like Altieri suggest a return to the practice of "three sisters" planting or crop rotation.

## Many Varieties of Corn

*Corn will grow almost anywhere in the United States. There are many varieties of corn plant. Sweet corn, such as corn on the cob, is often enjoyed by humans. Most American-grown corn, however, is hard, chewy field corn, also called dent corn. Pigs and other livestock eat field corn whole; people usually grind it up and cook it. Corn meal, grits, tortillas, corn bread, and corn flakes are all made from field corn. Popcorn is also made from field corn.*

### Growing Corn

**Materials:**
- A sunny patch of soil measuring 80 square meters (860 square feet)
- Corn seeds
- Water
- Fertilizer

**Directions:**
1. Wait until the danger of frost is over. Dig fertilizer into the soil and plant the corn seeds 5–10 centimeters (2–4 inches) apart in several short rows.
2. When the corn plants are about 15 centimeters (6 inches) tall, thin plants until they are 60–90 centimeters (2–3 feet) apart.
3. Keep the plants well watered. Fertilize every few weeks. Remove any weeds.
4. Your corn will be ready to eat in 2–3 months. Harvest the ears when the kernels are soft and plump.
5. Remove the husk and silk threads from each ear, boil, and enjoy!

Remember to annotate as you read.

Notes

# The Union of Corn and Bean

1     Long ago, when plants and animals had voices, a plant named Corn grew in a lovely garden. Corn was tall and handsome, and he had a thoughtful and generous spirit.

2     Most of the time, Corn was contented because he enjoyed his home and rejoiced in nature's beauty. Since he was tall, he had learned to be observant of his surroundings. Throughout the day, he liked to watch plants and animals going about their activities. *I have a good life,* Corn thought, *and I have no reason to complain.* Yet there were moments when his spirit was heavy, and he didn't understand why.

3     One evening, as Corn was enjoying the sunset, he saw two butterflies happily whispering and laughing. Suddenly, he understood why he felt unhappy at times. He was lonely and needed friendship and love. That night, Corn sang a song about his loneliness.

4     The following morning, a pretty Squash plant approached him. "I heard your song," she explained, "and I would happily live with you and marry you."

5     However, Corn realized that the two of them would not be a suitable match. "Although you are a splendid plant, we are not compatible," he replied. "You wander around the ground, while I remain in one spot, growing tall. Your large leaves block the sun from reaching smaller plants, while I prefer to share the sunlight."

6     Meanwhile, a Bean plant happened to overhear their conversation. She planted herself next to Corn, extending her vine around him. Corn and Bean grew tall together, and soon they were happily married. They promised never to part, which is why the Ottawa people plant corn and beans together, and grow squash nearby.

# BuildReflectWrite

## Build Knowledge

Answer the following questions based on this week's reading.

| A Short History of a Special Plant |
|---|
| **Why did the author include the section on Early Cultivation?** |
| **What is the purpose of the graph U.S. Corn Production?** |
| **What are some issues surrounding the growth and consumption of corn?** |

## Reflect

**How do we decide which resources we should develop?**

Based on this week's texts, write down new ideas and questions you have about the essential question.

_____

_____

_____

_____

_____

_____

## Building Research Skills

**Informative/Explanatory**

Imagine that you are conducting research to explain new ways to create ethanol. One of your guiding research questions is: Why do scientists think it is necessary to develop new ways to create ethanol? Read and take notes to gather facts and details from two or more sources to answer this question. List your sources.

Notes

# The Science of Growing Food

*Modern agriculture has changed the ecosystem. Farming technology has advanced and become more efficient. Yet, at what cost? Some farmers embrace the benefits of agricultural technology. Their critics, though, fear they are too focused on the bottom line and are losing sight of what truly benefits the soil. Read these two articles to hear opinions from both sides of the plow.*

## The Case for Keeping Corn Number 1

by Carla Corriols

1   Today, corn is the most widely grown crop in the United States. If Americans are smart, they'll keep it that way. At present, Americans are the most productive corn farmers in the world. They export an average of $10 billion worth of corn per year. According to the United States Department of Agriculture (USDA), corn is one of the few American products with a trade surplus.

2   Thanks to amazing new seed technology and other agricultural innovations, the corn grown on each acre may very well double again in only twenty-five years with continued support. This is good news for America and America's farmers.

Corn is a top crop for American growers.

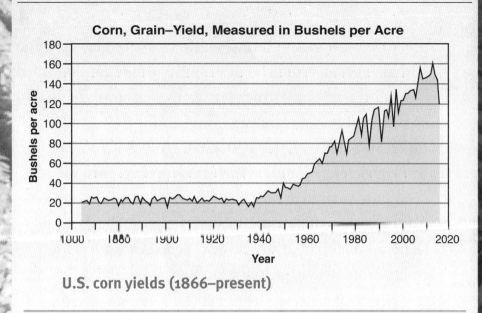

**Corn, Grain–Yield, Measured in Bushels per Acre**

**U.S. corn yields (1866–present)**

3    Corn crops dominate the American agricultural landscape for good reason. Mainly, corn is a productive crop. It has been bred and modified to produce astoundingly high yields compared with most other crops in the United States. Corn is an extremely resilient crop as well. It can flourish in a variety of climates. It not only thrives in the Midwest region, but also grows successfully in most other parts of the continental United States.

4    Corn is also highly versatile. Once grown, corn can be converted into a great number of marketable products. Sweet corn varieties can go directly from the farm to the table. It can be packaged into frozen and canned foods. Or, it can be processed and sold for human consumption in the form of corn flour, cornmeal, grits, corn tortillas, or corn syrup. Other breeds of corn can be grown and used to feed livestock, such as pigs, chickens, and cattle. Corn can also be turned into the biofuel called ethanol, or even into naturally biodegradable plastics.

5    In the past, Americans grew different crops to meet the needs of different markets. However, with the global economy and the availability of food crops from around the world, farmers no longer need to diversify as much. By consolidating crops and focusing efforts on corn, American growers have cut costs and become more efficient. We now lead the world in corn exports.

6    Some people are calling for a return to the more diversified farming practices of the past. They argue that soil is depleted by the two-crop corn-soybean rotation. However, science shows that plants get the majority of what they need to grow and repair themselves by combining water, air, and sunlight through photosynthesis. The high photosynthetic rate of corn plants means more organic matter is returned annually to the soil with corn than with other crops. New tillage methods have even reduced this soil loss, resulting in soil organic matter buildup with corn production. Corn also provides canopy protection to the soil surface. That reduces erosion caused by rainfall. Rotation with soybeans means nutrients can be restored to the soil, thus further preventing erosion. We must move forward with technology, not back in time!

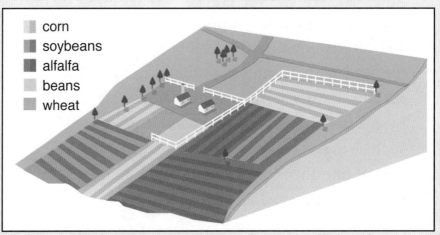

corn
soybeans
alfalfa
beans
wheat

**Farming multiple crops was more costly and inefficient for growers.**

**Today, precision farming is made possible by GPS technology.**

7    Over the last century, scientific breakthroughs in seed technology have allowed corn farmers to use genetically modified organisms, or GMOs, in farming. GMO corn has enabled farmers to grow five times more than they did in the 1930s on 20 percent less land. These seeds allow farmers to use fewer herbicides to kill weeds, and fewer pesticides to kill bugs.

8    Machines that use global positioning satellite, or GPS, technology have also allowed farmers to plant, feed, and water crops more precisely. That helps reduce waste and increase profits.

9    "We're more efficient than ever," says Nebraska corn farmer Jon Holzfaster. "We're using less fuel and traveling across the land fewer times. We have better genetics to help us optimize yields from existing acres. Our use of chemicals has decreased dramatically. . . . In this respect, the good old days are actually happening right now."

10   As a result of these breakthroughs in genetic and agricultural technology, corn crops generate billions per year for the American economy. It is the country's greatest agricultural export. By continuing to support America's corn industry, Americans will be investing in a bright future with enough food and fuel to power the world.

# Did Farmers of the Past Know More Than We Do?

by Verlyn Klinkenborg

*Editorial from the* New York Times, *November 3, 2012*

11    A couple years ago, I saw a small field of oats growing in northwest Iowa—a 40-acre patch in a sea of genetically modified corn and soybeans. It was an unusual sight. I asked my cousins, who still farm what my dad always called the "home place," whether someone had added oats to the rotation of crops being planted. The answer was no.

12    The purpose of that patch of oats was manure mitigation. The waste that had been sprayed on that field came from a hog confinement operation, and oats were the only crop that would put such concentrated, nearly toxic manure to nutritional use and do it quickly.

13    Oats used to be a common sight all over the Midwest. They were often sown with alfalfa as a "nurse crop" to provide some cover for alfalfa seedlings back when alfalfa was also a common sight. Until about thirty years ago, you could find all sorts of crops growing on Iowa farms, and livestock. Since then two things have happened. All the animals have moved indoors, into crowded confinement operations. And the number of crops has dwindled to exactly two: corn and soybeans.

Oats are shoveled into a conveyor's hopper at an Iowa farm in 1948, before corn and soybeans gained a near-monopoly on farmland.

14      My uncle Everon, who died last summer, farmed the home place when I was growing up. He would have been surprised to learn that he was following the principles of an early eighteenth-century agricultural experimenter named Charles Townshend, who, apart from his fascination with turnips, was every inch a viscount. Townshend's discovery—borrowed from Dutch and Flemish farmers—was that crops grow better, with fewer weeds and pest problems, if they are rotated in a careful sequence.

15      Townshend's rotation—like the ones George Washington and Thomas Jefferson used—included clover, wheat, other small grains and turnips, which made good winter food for sheep and cattle. My uncle grew no turnips, but he, like all his neighbors, was using his own version of the four-crop system, at the heart of which was alfalfa.

16      Getting to the four-crop rotation wasn't easy, historically speaking. The Romans knew about crop rotation, but by the Middle Ages, farming was based on the practice of letting the land lie fallow, unplanted—resting it, in other words. The purpose of that practice, like crop rotation itself, is to prevent the soil from becoming exhausted when the same crop is sown over and over again. In early American agriculture, only sophisticated farmers like Washington and Jefferson were using crop rotations in their fields. There was simply too much good land available. It was too easy to farm a piece and then move on when the soil was depleted.

17    In one sense, that is still how modern agriculture works. You look to the future and discard the past. A modern rotation includes only corn, soybeans, fertilizer, and pesticides. Whatever you may think about genetically modified crops, the switch to those varieties has driven the rush to the two-crop system. Those crops are designed to tolerate the presence of herbicides. The result is that farmland has been inundated with glyphosate, the herbicide genetically modified crops are engineered for.

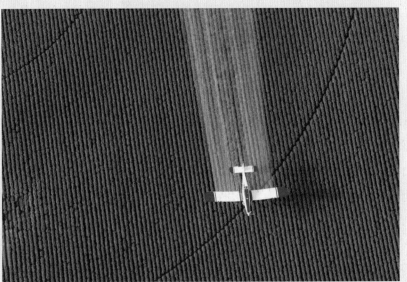

A crop duster sprays herbicide on genetically modified crops. Genetically modified crops are designed to tolerate herbicides.

18    The very structure of the agricultural system, as it stands now, is designed to return the greatest profit possible, not to the farmers but to the producers of the chemicals they use and the seeds they plant. And because those chemicals depend on fossil energy, the entire system is inherently unsustainable. What farmers used to return to the soil in the form of labor and animal manure—not the toxic kind you find in livestock confinement systems—they now must purchase, just the way they buy diesel for their tractors.

Notes

19     In fact, as a recent study by agronomists from the Department of Agriculture, Iowa State University and the University of Minnesota shows, there's nothing obsolete about four-crop rotation. It produces the same yields, it sharply reduces the toxicity of freshwater runoff, and it eliminates many of the problems associated with genetically modified crops, including the emergence of glyphosate-resistant weeds. It's also simply better for the soil. A four-crop rotation using conventional crop varieties, along with much lower applications of fertilizer and herbicides and some animal manure, works every bit as well as the prevailing monotony of corn and soybeans.

20     This study is a reminder of something essential. Modern agriculture is driven by diminishing biological diversity and relentless consolidation, from the farms themselves to the processors and the distributors of the crops and livestock. But you cannot consolidate the soil. It is a complex organism, and it always responds productively to diversity. The way we farm now undervalues and undermines good soil. Our idea of agricultural productivity and efficiency must include the ecological benefits of healthy soil. The surest way to improve the soil is to remember what industrial agriculture has chosen to forget.

**Crop rotation has both economic and environmental benefits.**

Remember to annotate as you read.

Notes

# The World's Only Corn Palace

1    Many palaces around the world have been built for kings and queens. However, there's only one palace that was built to celebrate corn. Located in Mitchell, South Dakota, the middle of America, it's the one and only Corn Palace.

2    The Corn Palace looks like a Russian castle. Inside and out, it's decorated with large, colorful murals made of corn, grain, and grass. At first glance, the murals look like mosaics made of small tiles. On closer inspection, though, you see that they're made of different colored corn!

3    The murals on the outside of the building are changed yearly to reflect different themes. For example, past themes have been "Everyday Heroes and America's Destinations." The murals inside the palace are changed about every ten years.

4    All the corn used in these incredible murals is grown by local farmers. They plant corn in a variety of colors, including several shades of red and brown, as well as blue, white, black, orange, and green.

5    Each year, local artists make sketches for the outside murals. Once the sketches are done, they are put on huge rolls of tar paper and tacked on the building. Then the ears of corn are nailed into place. It's like completing a puzzle or painting by numbers.

6    About 500,000 people visit the Corn Palace each year to see the unforgettable artwork. The best time to visit is between May and September. Once winter starts, local birds begin to nibble on the murals. That's when the Corn Palace is also called the World's Largest Bird Feeder!

# BuildReflectWrite

## Build Knowledge

Use the chart below to record information you learned this week about different problems corn growers face—and solutions to those problems. Include more than one solution when possible.

| Problem | Solution |
| --- | --- |
|  |  |

## Reflect

**How do we decide which resources we should develop?**

Based on this week's texts, write down new ideas and questions you have about the essential question.

_____

_____

_____

_____

_____

_____

## Building Research Skills

**Opinion**

In "The Science of Growing Food," you read about two approaches to planting crops. Farmers can use modern technology to focus on one crop year after year, or they can use a traditional system of crop rotation. Imagine that you have been asked to do research in order to write an opinion essay on which approach is better. One of your guiding research questions is: What are the benefits of using crop rotation? Read and take notes from two or more print or digital sources to find facts and details to help you formulate your opinion. List the sources you use.

# Support for Collaborative Conversation

## Discussion Prompts

### Express ideas or opinions . . .

When I read _____, it made me think that _____.

Based on the information in _____, my [opinion/idea] is _____.

As I [listened to/read/watched] _____, it occurred to me that _____.

It was important that _____.

### Gain the floor . . .

I would like to add a comment. _____.

Excuse me for interrupting, but _____.

That made me think of _____.

### Build on a peer's idea or opinion . . .

That's an interesting point. It makes me think _____.

If _____, then maybe _____.

[Name] said _____. That could mean that _____.

### Express agreement with a peer's idea . . .

I agree that _____ because _____.

I also feel that _____ because _____.

[Name] made the comment that _____, and I think that is important because _____.

### Respectfully express disagreement . . .

I understand your point of view that _____, but in my opinion _____ because _____.

That is an interesting idea, but did you consider the fact that _____?

I do not agree that _____. I think that _____ because _____.

### Ask a clarifying question . . .

You said _____. Could you explain what you mean by that?

I don't understand how your evidence supports that inference. Can you say more?

I'm not sure I understand. Are you saying that _____?

### Clarify for others . . .

When I said _____, what I meant was that _____.

I reached my conclusion because _____.

## Group Roles

**Discussion director:**
Your role is to guide the group's discussion and be sure that everyone has a chance to express his or her ideas.

**Notetaker:**
Your job is to record the group's ideas and important points of discussion.

**Summarizer:**
In this role, you will restate the group's comments and conclusions.

**Presenter:**
Your role is to provide an overview of the group's discussion to the class.

**Timekeeper:**
You will track the time and help keep your peers on task.

# Making Meaning with Words

| Word | My Definition | My Sentence |
|---|---|---|
| **beneficial** (p. 13) | | |
| **consumption** (p. 7) | | |
| **cultivated** (p. 4) | | |
| **depleting** (p. 9) | | |
| **diversify** (p. 24) | | |
| **dominate** (p. 23) | | |
| **emergence** (p. 7) | | |
| **generate** (p. 7) | | |
| **principles** (p. 18) | | |
| **surplus** (p. 13) | | |
| | | |

Lexile 850L–1110L

# Build Knowledge Across 10 Topic Strands

**Government and Citizenship**

The U.S. Constitution: **Then and Now**

**Character**

Developing **Characters' Relationships**

**Life Science**

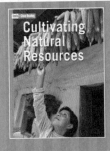

**Cultivating Natural Resources**

**Point of View**

Recognizing **Author's Point of View**

**Technology and Society**

Technology's **Impact** on Society

**Theme**

**Up Against** *the* **Wild**

**History and Culture**

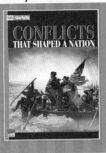

**CONFLICTS THAT SHAPED A NATION**

**Earth Science**

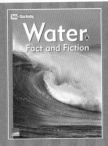

**Water** Fact and Fiction

**Economics**

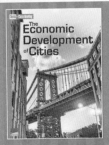

The **Economic Development** of Cities

**Physical Science**

Transforming **Matter**

Grade 5 • Unit 3

ISBN 978-1-4900-9207

Benchmark UNIVERSE.COM™

BENCHMARK EDUCATION COMPANY

9 781490 092072